A ONE-ACT PLAY

No Fading Star

By
CELESTE RASPANTI

THE DRAMATIC PUBLISHING COMPANY

*** NOTICE ***

NO FADING STAR

A One-Act Play

For 4 Men, 5 Women, Extras

C H A R A C T E R S

MOTHER FRANZISKA *Mother Superior of Convent*
SISTER KLARA . . . .*Her assistant*
KLAAS SHOEFFLER . . . . *Worker for convent*
DAVID SACHS . . . . *Jewish child brought to convent*
MIRIAM SACHS . . . .*His sister*
SERGEANT HEIMLICH . . . . *Nazi sergeant*
SSTER MONIKA . . . . *Sister in charge of kitchen*
SL MOELLER . . . . *Franziska's sister, married to Nazi*
COLONEL LAUBER . . . . *Nazi commander*

OTHER CHILDREN

Time: The Holocaust

Place: A Convent, near Baden

3

INTRODUCTORY NOTE

There is documentary evidence in the testimony of
Jews, who as children, were saved from the Holocaust
through the efforts of religious women in the convents
of Germany and other Nazi occupied countries . . .
This play is dedicated to these nameless women and
the good people who worked with them to write some
few bright words in the dark history of the Holocaust.

The first production of NO FADING STAR was pre-
sented at Centre Stage, Minneapolis, under the direc-
tion of Stephen Phillips.

For Robert G. Pitman

19 -1978

Actor, Director, Friend

NO FADING STAR

Scene: The stage is set with platforms indicating areas of action. UC, silhouetted against the sky, an escape to the border. DR, the office in the convent of Maria Morgenstern, Mary, the Morning Star, near the town of Baden, not too far from the French Border. The chapel of the convent is merely indicated UL when the nuns are at prayer. Other areas of action exist when lighted in the C area. At rise, several nuns are in the chapel just concluding morning prayers. The *Salve Regina*, the traditional anthem that concludes the service, is heard. DSR a fire is burning in the stove.

MOTHER FRANZISKA (feeding the contents of a file drawer into the fire, which seems for a moment to blaze out of control and light up the stage). There! There's the last. (The chapel bell starts to chime slowly; the early morning service has ended.) ~~And in time for . . . another day.~~

SISTER KLARA. Good morning, Mother.

MOTHER FRANZISKA. Good morning, Sister Klara - do you see that glorious sun coming up, and the morning star fading? It makes me want to nudge that old bell a little - and let it ring - with a little less dignity.

SISTER KLARA. It's hundreds of years old - it rings a lot of memories . . .

7

MOTHER FRANZISKA. Yes, I suppose. But so much
        dignity - I cherish this friendly old sound, bold
        and happy. (She takes an old school bell from
        the desk and rings it loudly.) There, that's the
        way to ring in the sun.
SISTER KLARA. Yes, but . . .
MOTHER FRANZISKA. Well, Sister, it may be the
        only cause for smiling we have this day, please,
        try, please . . .
SISTER KLARA (a weak smile). Mother, Klaus Hoef-
        fler is here - with a truckload of supplies -
        flour, bolts of linen, and the rest of the things
        we asked for.
MOTHER FRANZISKA. And you frowning? Thank
        God, we can stop counting out peas and beans
        - and do better with the soup tonight, though
        Sister Monika does well - with what she has
        I will admit. Why the frown?
SISTER KLARA. He's brought - children - again, two
        children.
MOTHER FRANZISKA. Children? And only two?
        Well . . . now that the school is closed, we'll
        have to say, to say . . . they're . . . the nieces
        of Herr Dokter Schneider. He'll claim them
        until we can get them out.
SISTER KLARA. Yes, Mother, but these children -
        you call them - Herr Doktor's nieces - I don't
        think anyone will believe that . . . you see . . .
MOTHER FRANZISKA. Of course they will. We've
        done that many times before.
SISTER KLARA. Well . . . you'll see. (She turns to
        go.) Mother, I don't know how we can

continue . . . last week . . . three times . . .

MOTHER FRANZISKA. Yes, I know, the searches, ~~unannounced.~~ Since the order came to close, we're being watched, ~~I'm sure.~~ It may be that we've come to the end of our usefulness, at least with the children, but . . .

SISTER KLARA. Klaas is growling again. He hears what they say in town, and he's been warned.

MOTHER FRANZISKA. By whom?

SISTER KLARA. Well, by Herr Doktor Schneider, for one. Kurt Frieberg said they announced the last search of the ghetto.

MOTHER FRANZISKA. I've taken some precautions. I've burned the records. ~~Any notes, forms, anything at all that will give proof that - black on white - the children in the school were not who we said they were.~~

~~SISTER KLARA. The birth certific~~ates?

MOTHER FRANZISKA. If they find any trace that we've been creating false documents, they'll search even further. So I've burned them all.

KLAAS (breaking in). Mother Franziska, Sister Klara, I won't wait any longer - while you two stand here gossiping. ~~Ach, my feet hurt, my back aches.~~ I've been out to the farm before dawn, and I won't wait.

MOTHER FRANZISKA. Of course not. Klaas, my dear scowling friend, come in here and growl a bit at me. It makes my day complete.

KLAAS. Well, now, it's just that I . . .

MOTHER FRANZISKA. It's just that you're tired. You've been out to the mill and the farm,

~~you've haggled for the flour and the meat,~~ and
now you can sit here for a few minutes and
growl at me. Sister Klara, there must be a cup
of hot coffee, real coffee, ~~not that ersatz brew
we've been drinking, real coffee~~ in the kitchen
for Klaas.

SISTER KLARA. With a pinch of sugar, if Sister
Monika can spare some. (She leaves.)

KLAAS. ~~That's better.~~ I tell you, Mother Franziska,
I'm not able to do this much longer. ~~I can't
keep up the pace -- loading the sacks, driving
half the night, most of the day, bargaining and
conniving to get what we need here for . . .~~

MOTHER FRANZISKA. ~~For the work that must be
done here.~~ It's hard, so hard, dear friend, I
know.

KLAAS. ~~Oh, I suppose I complain a lot, but what can
I do, what can any of us do?~~ Last night in the
town, another search and . . . (Suddenly solemn.)
There are two children in the truck, ~~two more,~~
and I'm afraid . . .

MOTHER FRANZISKA. Sister Klara told me. Yesterday, I had decided, ~~almost,~~ after last week's
random searches -- I had almost decided to stop
for a while. Kurt tells me the Gestapo is savage
in its searches of the wagons and trucks. But
now, when the children are here -- how can we
refuse them? We can take them in as the nieces
of Herr Doktor Schneider. He's helped us in
the past; he'll do that for us again.

KLAAS. ~~Claim them?~~ Ach, Mother Franziska, you
mean he'll tell a little lie for us.

MOTHER FRANZISKA. Now, Klaas, it's really not a
lie -- we've been through this before, you and I.
~~For the Herr Doktor to claim one or the other~~
~~of the children here as his nieces -- well, it's~~ not
really a lie. ~~For all we know, with the families~~
~~and cousins in and about Baden, so many rela-~~
~~tives~~ -- he may very well be an uncle, a distant
uncle of the children ~~... he may very well be.~~

KLAAS. Yes, yes, I know the argument. Somewhere
in the distant past, we are all related, and the
Gestapo has not time to climb the family trees
of "respectable" citizens like Herr Doktor and
the nuns at Maria Morgenstern.

MOTHER FRANZISKA. ~~And Klaas Hoeffler.~~ You've
been an uncle more times than you know --
~~than I have remembered to tell you.~~ It's what
I call -- an honest deception -- do you know
what I mean?

KLAAS (with good humor). Yes, and the birth certificates and the Aryan passports -- all honest
deceptions.

MOTHER FRANZISKA. Yes, and the "nieces" of
Herr Doktor, two girls in the novitiate of
Maria Morgenstern. They'll leave them alone.

KLAAS. But there's just one thing . . .

MOTHER FRANZISKA. Yes?

KLAAS. One of these nieces is a nephew!

MOTHER FRANZISKA. A boy? Oh, I was not ex-
pecting that . . ~~but~~ well, we shall have
to work that out. We won't turn him away.

KLAAS. You may not have a chance. He may run
away; he's an angry fellow! What are you
laughing at?

MOTHER FRANZISKA. A boy in the novitiate!
Klaas, it's actually amusing. A boy! Well, we'll
work it out.

KLAAS. Perhaps, but this time, these must be the last.
After last week, we'll jeopardize the whole
group, those who are even now on their way to
the border. I swore Monday night, no more,
no more. But these two, I could not refuse.

SISTER KLARA (returning). Here, here is a good hot
cup of strong coffee for you -- with a little
pinch of sugar. And from Sister Monika in the
kitchen -- kuchen!

KLAAS. Ah, kuchen! It's a bribe, that's certain, a
bribe. But, ah, what an aroma!

MOTHER FRANZISKA. Klaas Hoeffler, you are
shamelessly corruptible, a slice of kuchen!
You'd sell your soul.

KLAAS. I would, I would. (Eating heartily.)

MOTHER FRANZISKA. No, Sister, just a cup of
coffee for me. And tell Sister Monika that
Klaas will be stopping in the kitchen to unload
the supplies. Perhaps she can reinforce this
bribe with a loaf of fresh bread for Marta and
the girls.

KLAAS. I'm obliged to you, Sister Klara. I'll stop in
the kitchen -- you can warn Sister Monika.

SISTER KLARA (leaving). Oh, don't worry, she'll be
ready for you.

MOTHER FRANZISKA. Now, the children.

KLAAS. Gerda Sachs -- you remember?

MOTHER FRANZISKA. Gerda? Yes, of course, but
I thought she had left Germany. Gerda -- we

were best friends.

KLAAS. They've been called. Last week the Gestapo
broke down the door and arrested Martin.
~~Things had been quiet in the ghetto for the~~
~~last weeks, but without warning, without~~
~~reason~~

MOTHER FRANZISKA. ~~Reason?~~

KLAAS. ~~They broke down the door~~ and took him
for questioning, they said. But he's not returned and Gerda hears that he -- he's on the
train. Then yesterday, Gerda . . .

MOTHER FRANZISKA. My God, ~~Gerda and Martin!~~

KLAAS. You see why my feet are dragging -- one by
one, our friends, but Martin -- such good
friends -- and nothing can be done.

MOTHER FRANZISKA. We do what we can.

KLAAS. ~~Oh, sometimes I remember~~ -- at first, the
stars. The shame of it. I couldn't look Martin
in the eye. But even he, he used to say -- 'Ach,
this will be the end of it -- the stars, the ghetto
– the war will be over -- so it goes.' ~~Even~~ he
didn't know all this would happen.

MOTHER FRANZISKA. But who could have imagined
the hate -- and the power of that hate. And
now, we must do what we can . . . we must
save the children. ~~Take some comfort, friend,~~
~~we do what we can.~~

KLAAS. The children, ~~yes, the children.~~ Gerda has
asked me -- this letter, from her. (He hands
her a letter.)

MOTHER FRANZISKA (opens it slowly). 'Dear
Fritzie,' (To KLAAS.) She is the only one

of all my friends who still calls me that.
Fritzie! She'll never change ... (She continues
with the letter, interrupting now and then to
include KLAAS.) 'Dear Fritzie, Forgive me,
for I take your life into my hands as I write
this letter. We are the last to leave Ludwig-
strasse, the last Jews.' I suppose Martin's work
at the clinic kept them there. She says they've
burned the school and the synagogue and ...
here, she says, 'It seems we are all being swept
into flames that will destroy us.' The Sterns
and the Rosens have gone and she, she must
have written this just before leaving. She says,
'Lisl, your dear Lisl, has changed so, we dare
not approach her.' Oh, and here, she says,
'Except for Klaas and Marta and the Friebergs,
we are alone.'

KLAAS. Yes, we shared what we had ... and I promised to bring the children here.

MOTHER FRANZISKA (continues to read). 'I am
sending my children to you -- David and
Miriam -- save them for me -- for all of us. I
cannot bear to think that they will perish in
the flames. Your friend, Gertie.' (She pauses
to glance over the letter again, turns the page.)
Oh, here, a note, "David will be thirteen next
week. He would have been Bar Mitzvah this
Sabbath ...' (She folds the letter slowly.)
My dear, dear Gertie ... (She throws it on the
table.) And my poor sister Lisl!

KLAAS. Poor? A fool! That's what! (Hesitant.) Perhaps I shouldn't say so, Mother Franziska, but

> you know me as an honest man, and I say, I say Lisl is a . . .

MOTHER FRANZISKA. She's a fool, Klaas, and it's pitiful that she destroys everything she knows to be right in her foolishness, but she's my sister and she's a grown woman. I despise what she stands for -- and yet, I still grieve for what she is.

KLAAS. I'm sorry, but it's the truth. No one trusts her. The people in town know she's a sympathizer -- and though they respect you, and the memory of your good father and mother, they will not give her a crumb of sympathy -- or friendliness.

MOTHER FRANZISKA. What can I say? Married to Captain Moeller, she makes her choice to stand against us -- her friends and family. She knows how I feel, avoids me -- and it's just as well. I don't want her here, asking questions, seeing what she should not see -- or hearing. It's just as well. She would not understand . . . any of this. That we could not face the living God -- or ourselves if we did not, as dear Gerda says -- take our lives into our own hands.

KLAAS. What Gerda said was -- *she*, Gerda, *she* takes *your* life into *her* hands -- you are no longer ignorant of her. She is right. She takes your life into her hands.

MOTHER FRANZISKA. Klaas, tonight -- will you make another trip, notify the Friebergs?

KLAAS. Do you hear me? I say, she is right, she takes your life and the lives of all of us, the nuns, the few sick who are still here -- the whole monastery, Maria Morgenstern -- here for hundreds of years -- she takes it all into her hands -- with a letter -- evidence. If Heimlich and the Gestapo come again . . . they will not leave alone.

MOTHER FRANZISKA. Yes, I'm afraid that's true. Kurt warned me yesterday that they would be making unannounced visits any day. I burned all the records -- all the papers.

KLAAS (trying to understand). She takes your life . . .

MOTHER FRANZISKA (with resolution). No! No, I take my life into *my own* hands! My life -- the sisters, the monastery, all of it -- you and I -- and they -- all of it -- in my hands! It's too late! (She picks up the letter and with one last look, throws it into the fire.) But the children, they will not be destroyed! (Gently.) Klaas, my dear friend Klaas, will you work, will you stay with us in this work?

KLAAS. Yes, what else can I do?

MOTHER FRANZISKA. Now, where are the children?

(LIGHTS GO DOWN as MOTHER FRANZISKA begins to set things in order. LIGHTS COME UP DIMLY on the two children huddled together.)

DAVID. Miriam, it's all right. Klaas will come back -- and you have to stay here.

MIRIAM. Why? I want to go with you.

DAVID. Please, Miriam, you must stay here. I have to go. I'm not going to hide here like, like a -- little boy, hide in a convent!

MIRIAM. But where are you going to go?

DAVID. I'm going to try to get out -- and back to
      Baden -- with the others. I have to go! I must
      go! Miriam, please . . .

MIRIAM. I want to go with you!

DAVID. Please, you don't understand. I'm -- the only
      one left -- I have to go. Here, you take the
      sweater and the scarf that Mama packed, you
      take these things. (He unpacks the bundle for
      her.) This'll keep you warm.

MIRIAM. But what about you?

DAVID. Don't be afraid. They'll take care of you --
      you can stay here, hide here in the convent --
      a girl -- you can hide, but I must go . . . What's
      that? (KLAAS stomps his foot twice, a signal.)
      Here, behind the trunk. Here, depend on me

KLAAS (entering). There you are. Why did you move
      from the truck -- until you were told?

DAVID. I'm not afraid.

KLAAS. Well, I am.

MOTHER FRANZISKA (coming out of the darkness
      behind KLAAS). And so am I.

DAVID. I'm going to leave here -- now.

KLAAS. It's not safe now, maybe not even tonight --
      you'll have to wait.

DAVID. I don't believe you . . . (To MOTHER
      FRANZISKA.) Who are you?

MOTHER FRANZISKA. Mother Franziska, your
      mother's good friend.

DAVID. How do I know?

KLAAS. You know because she tells you; that's how
      you know!

MOTHER FRANZISKA. Yes, you can believe me --

I am your mother's friend.

DAVID. Friend? Jews don't have friends -- not here --
in such a place!

MOTHER FRANZISKA. Your mother and I went to
school together, to the university -- years ago.

DAVID. Jews don't go to school with . . . gentiles . . .
Christians!

MOTHER FRANZISKA. It hasn't always been like it
is now, David. Believe me, it was not always
like this. We went to school, Gertie and I, to
the university -- and we were in the band together. Your mother played the flute, and I --
I tried to play the clarinet.

MIRIAM. You called Mama, Gertie? Papa calls her
that.

MOTHER FRANZISKA. Yes, and she calls me,
Fritzie. My name is Franziska, and when I was
a girl, my friends, but good friends only, called
me Fritzie -- your mother, she still calls me that.

DAVID. You're just saying that.

MOTHER FRANZISKA. I was your mother's good
friend. She met your father at the university
and they married. I came to Maria Morgenstern. And you've been here, too.

DAVID. I don't remember. You're just saying that.

MOTHER FRANZISKA. When you were a small
child, when the whole town celebrated a great
anniversary of Maria Morgenstern, you were
here. You were a very little boy and you
marched with the other children from the
town in a parade. It was a very big party for
all of us.

DAVID. I don't remember

KLAAS. Well, she remembers! And she's telling the
        truth. She, we, all of us -- we know Martin and
        Gerda Sachs. We've risked our lives to help.
        Believe that!

DAVID (starts to separate his things from MIRIAM's
        in the bundle.) I have to go. I can't stay here.
        It's important that I go back to Baden.

KLAAS. It's not safe. We've risked our lives to help
        -- and you can't go back, now that you're here.

MOTHER FRANZISKA. We have a way to help -- but
        it grows more dangerous every day. We're
        watched. The Gestapo -- makes searches any
        time. We must be careful not to take foolish
        risks. To let you go back -- would be a foolish
        risk.

DAVID. I didn't ask to come here.

MOTHER FRANZISKA. Perhaps not, but you're here.

DAVID. But only for Miriam.

MOTHER FRANZISKA. I'm sure she appreciates
        that. Come here, Miriam. You know, Miriam,
        you were here too, that same spring day.

MIRIAM. I remember.

MOTHER FRANZISKA. Oh, do you?

DAVID. You were only a baby . . . you don't remem-
        ber!

MOTHER FRANZISKA. Yes, you were only a baby
        -- but I remember it all very well. And I'm so
        glad you're here now. How old are you,
        Miriam?

DAVID. She's eight, I think.

MIRIAM. I'm almost nine.

MOTHER FRANZISKA. And you're quite tall for
~~almost~~ nine.

DAVID. And I'm thirteen.

MOTHER FRANZISKA. Going to be thirteen next
week?

DAVID. I'm thirteen -- and old enough to be . . .

MOTHER FRANZISKA. Bar Mitzvah?

DAVID. How do you know about Bar Mitzvah?

MOTHER FRANZISKA. Oh, I know. And I know
that you were to be Bar Mitzvah this Sabbath.

DAVID. Yes, but now . . . that's why I have to return.
It's important. I'm the last.

MOTHER FRANZISKA. There's every chance that
you will get to the border, safe.

DAVID. But I want to be with . . . Jews, my people.
I should be Bar Mitzvah.

MOTHER FRANZISKA. Are you prepared?

DAVID. Yes, I've been getting ready for a long time,
secretly. I read the Torah with Father -- I
prepared. That's why I must go back, you see.
I must go back for my Bar Mitzvah.

KLAAS. There's nothing to go back to ~~-- there's no
one there -- there couldn't be any Bar Mitzvah~~.
Do you think they wouldn't find a boy alone --
in the ghetto? Your Mother wrote to us . . .
~~There's nothing to go back to -- for you.~~

DAVID. Then I have to go to be with my people.

MOTHER FRANZISKA. Even if it means -- that you
will go with the rest to the East -- to work?

DAVID. Work? You don't believe that, do you? We
know. But even then, I would be with my
people, not hiding, like a child. ~~I want to go,~~

please, let me go. If you'll take care of Miriam,
then I'm free to go.

MOTHER FRANZISKA. We'll take care of Miriam --
but, first, let me look at you. Greasy clothes,
a dirty face . . . and your hand is bleeding.

DAVID. It's nothing. I scratched it on the side of the
truck.

KLAAS. He looks like he could use a good meal, too.
They've been hiding in the bottom of the truck
most of the night. Are you hungry?

DAVID. I'm not hungry -- please, I have to go.

MOTHER FRANZISKA. Klaas, will you ask Sister
Klara to bring some first aid supplies? And
something to eat . . . oh, and ask Sister Monika
to find a slice of apple kuchen, too -- even if
she has to make a miracle.

KLAAS (leaving). Well, it'll take a miracle -- that's
certain!

DAVID. I'm not . . . hungry. Please, I must go back.
I promised -- my father, I must be Bar Mitzvah.

MOTHER FRANZISKA. Ah, Martin, you promised
him. I think he would understand -- there isn't
any way for that to happen -- even if you did
return.

DAVID. I promised him I would stand and say to
anyone -- I am a Jew. I will not hide I am a
Jew, and I will stand like a man.

MOTHER FRANZISKA. David, you will keep your
promise. After a little rest, a bath -- right now,
I'm afraid the Gestapo would smell you before
they saw you -- a bath, and a look at that rusty
cut -- and a slice of apple kuchen -- perhaps we

can talk about your Bar Mitzvah - - here.

DAVID (cautious, but interested). Here?

MOTHER FRANZISKA. Stranger things have hap-
        pened here, believe me, David. ~~Believe.~~

DAVID. You're just saying that . . .

MOTHER FRANZISKA. No, I'm not just saying that.
        Believe me. ~~We have had Passover here -- and
        we have sung Kaddish for the dead. Believe
        me, we~~ will find a way, a little makeshift, per-
        haps. But you will have your Bar Mitzvah.
        ~~You will stand like a man to say, unashamed --
        that you are a Jew. I promise.~~

DAVID (takes off his jacket, rearranges the bundles,
        relaxes against the trunk). Well, I can wait --
        a little then.

MOTHER FRANZISKA. Good. Sister Klara will be
        here soon. ~~Rest while you wait.~~ (She leaves,
        taking MIRIAM with her.)

DAVID (leans back and rests, almost asleep). Mother
        Franziska!

MOTHER FRANZISKA (out of sight, but answers
        from the darkness). Yes?

DAVID. Do you think Sister Monika can really make
        a miracle -- I mean about the kuchen? ~~I am
        hungry!~~

(BLACKOUT)

(MOTHER FRANZISKA returns to her office to work
        at the desk. She is disturbed by voices from
        the kitchen.)

SERGEANT HEIMLICH. Heil Hitler! Sergeant
          Heimlich here. I have a message for Mother
          Franziska from the office of the Gestapo in
          Baden.

SISTER MONIKA. She is busy -- just a moment -- you
          will not track up my kitchen with those dirty
          boots.

MOTHER FRANZISKA (calling). Sister Monika, what
          is it?

SISTER MONIKA (entering with the guard). It's
          Sergeant Heimlich, from the Gestapo, in Baden.
          He walked through my clean kitchen with his
          dirty boots -- and I won't have it.

HEIMLICH (obsequious). My deepest apologies,
          Sister. The business of the Gestapo doesn't
          seem as important to you as a clean floor. I
          assure you it is.

SISTER MONIKA. I have no business with the Gesta-
          po! (She leaves.)

HEIMLICH (bowing). Sister Monika, she is always
          the same. I can predict what she will say, a
          simple soul . . .

MOTHER FRANZISKA. In a way. She speaks the
          truth as she sees it. What can I do for you,
          Sergeant?

HEIMLICH. Orders from Colonel Lauber, to search
          here. He believes you can be of assistance to
          the Gestapo.

MOTHER FRANZISKA. I doubt it.

HEIMLICH. The Jews have at last left Baden.

MOTHER FRANZISKA. Assisted by the Gestapo?

HEIMLICH. But within the last few weeks, months

really, we have become increasingly aware that
-- perhaps they have been getting assistance
from others, and have . . . emigrated . . . to
other places, have avoided reporting . . . for
work . . .

MOTHER FRANZISKA. Yes, yes, go on . . .

HEIMLICH. I have recently been assigned, promoted,
and assigned . . .

MOTHER FRANZISKA. So I have noticed.

HEIMLICH. I have been promoted because I have
been able to keep the town quite calm and . . .
I know the people, the Jews here, ~~and know
how to deal with them.~~ I know what needs to
be done to keep them under . . .

MOTHER FRANZISKA. Control?

HEIMLICH. In order. But . . . (He is very uncomfortable.) There are rumors, people in Baden have
reported seeing Jews in this vicinity, and on
the orders of Colonel Lauber, I am to . . .
search . . .

MOTHER FRANZISKA (exasperated). Manny Heimlich! You are talking to the woman who
treated your acne three years ago -- and sent
you off with a scolding -- and an apple when
you climbed our orchard walls. ~~I'm a busy
woman and have my work with the sick --
and the monastery of Maria Morgenstern.~~ I
have no time for your posturings.

HEIMLICH (disarmed). Mother Franziska, I have
been charged, my superior officer ~~has charged
me,~~ has instructed me to search the premises.

MOTHER FRANZISKA. Premises! This is the House

of God, not public premises to be violated.
Go to your superior officer and tell him you
have the word of the prioress of the monastery
of Maria Morgenstern -- you will find only the
sick here -- and very few of them remain.

HEIMLICH. But . . . I must search; that is my order
from Colonel Lauber.

MOTHER FRANZISKA (concluding the meeting).
Good day! That is my message to Colonel
Lauber.

HEIMLICH (with military precision). I will return
later and you will not send me away. Good
day. Heil Hitler!

MOTHER FRANZISKA (waiting until he is gone).
Sister Klara, Sister Monika, will you come
here, please?

SISTER KLARA (entering). Yes, what is it? Miriam
and David have eaten -- but they're so tired.
Do you think it is wise for them to travel?

MOTHER FRANZISKA. No, but we'll have to get
them both out tonight -- as early as possible.

SISTER KLARA. Yes . . . But both the children are
sleeping on their feet --

MOTHER FRANZISKA. Sergeant Heimlich -- ~~Manny~~
~~Heimlich~~, you saw him?

SISTER KLARA. I heard Sister Monika scolding him
in the kitchen -- about his boots. He's come
with a unit to make a search?

MOTHER FRANZISKA. Not yet -- at least not for
now, but soon. He'll be back, and we must
get the children out with Klaas to the Friebergs. They'll have to hide there until tonight.

SISTER MONIKA (entering). I've just now finished
        emptying the sacks -- a blessing between us
        and hunger. Mother, we must find a way to
        give the sick more milk.
MOTHER FRANZISKA. We will; we will. But you
        do very well, Sister. Klaas swears you make
        miracles.
SISTER MONIKA. In a way, I suppose. But I can
        only do so much -- skimping here and there.
        But with milk . . .
MOTHER FRANZISKA. You're right, the patients
        need more milk. We'll find a way, but first . . .
SISTER KLARA. First we have to do something
        about the children.
SISTER MONIKA. The Sachs children? Klaas told
        me.
MOTHER FRANZISKA. Sergeant Heimlich . . .
SISTER MONIKA (interrupting). Sergeant Heimlich!
        A few years ago he was stealing apples from
        the west orchard! A uniform makes big
        courage in small men!
MOTHER FRANZISKA. That's just it! He's
        threatened now and he'll be back -- with
        Colonel Lauber to back him up. We won't
        be able to get rid of him so quickly.
SISTER KLARA. The children will have to leave
        then -- as soon as possible.
SISTER MONIKA. The infirmary? There are
        enough empty beds there.
MOTHER FRANZISKA. No, the Gestapo will not
        expect to find sick children -- they would
        suspect. They must leave.

SISTER KLARA. They'll need papers.

MOTHER FRANZISKA. I'll prepare papers for them, ~~Aryan papers~~ -- new names, birth and baptismal certificates. Klaas must get word to the Friebergs, ~~that they will be coming and will need to hide -- at least through the night~~. If they leave here early evening -- Vespers, perhaps, they should have enough darkness to get them to the farm.

SISTER MONIKA. And what will we do with the Gestapo if they come before Vespers?

MOTHER FRANZISKA. We'll take a chance that they'll come later -- and if they do not . . .

SISTER MONIKA. I'll scrub the kitchen again, and keep them at bay with my mop and pail.

MOTHER FRANZISKA. I wish it were so easy, but do what you can to help.

SISTER KLARA. I'll get them ready . . .

MOTHER FRANZISKA. Yes . . . wait . . . there's one thing more. David . . . He's struggling . . .

SISTER KLARA. Yes, he's confused and angry. ~~Many come here with great and painful anger, Mother.~~

MOTHER FRANZISKA. I promised him, perhaps I shouldn't have -- but I did -- it seemed so important to him . . .

SISTER KLARA. Promised him?

MOTHER FRANZISKA. Yes, I promised him that -- ~~if we could -- if there was any way --~~

SISTER MONIKA. He wants to go back, even with his mouth filled with kuchen -- ~~eyes bigger than his stomach~~ -- he says he wants to go back. You didn't promise him that?

MOTHER FRANZISKA. No, not that he would go
back, but that -- he could be . . . Bar Mitzvah
here . . .

SISTER KLARA. You promised?

MOTHER FRANZISKA. It's important -- more than
ever now, I'm sure. It's important for him to
. . . be a Jew.

SISTER KLARA. But even if there were time, there
would be no chance to bring a Rabbi here.
You know there is no Rabbi in Baden any more.

MOTHER FRANZISKA. Well, we would have to make
some changes . . . I think he understands that,
but for him to stand and say that he is a Jew . . .
that's important.

SISTER MONIKA. This evening at Vespers?

MOTHER FRANZISKA. Yes, tonight at Vespers, in
the light of the evening star, he will read the
lesson from the Old Testament before all of
us . . . speak his own words to us . . . and after
that, go with Klaas.

SISTER KLARA. Well, there should be time for that.

MOTHER FRANZISKA. Before the whole community, he
this boy, this young man, David Sachs -- will
stand -- and in the presence of God -- and all
of us -- he will say he is a Jew and a Son of the
Law. This is all we can do. As for the Ritual
. . . it is in his heart. It's all we can do . . . but
it will be something.

SISTER MONIKA. So, tonight, at the hour of the
evening star, as it fades . . .

MOTHER FRANZISKA. No! No fading star, but

David's star. I promised. With the closing
hymn the children can leave with Klaas, behind the altar and up through the back.
SISTER KLARA. By the Time the *Salve* is ended,
they will be outside the wall, safe.
MOTHER FRANZISKA. I hope so. And after that,
the Vesper bell. When we hear the Vesper
bells ring -- ~~when we hear that,~~ then there'll
be time for rejoicing. (She returns to her desk,
preparing to work on papers for the children.
SISTER KLARA and SISTER MONIKA leave.
There is a distant bell and in the dim light,
LISL MOELLER, MOTHER FRANZISKA's
sister, enters.)
LISL (entering). Franziska -- I ~~must certainly be in~~-
truding -- ~~but I couldn't wait outside.~~
MOTHER FRANZISKA (caught unawares at her
work). Ah, Lisl, you see, as usual I am at my
desk. I wish I had known you were coming,
I would have come to meet you.
LISL. Oh, I know my way through these corridors
-- I'm not a stranger.
MOTHER FRANZISKA. In ~~a~~ way you are. How
long has it been? Months? ~~Yes, months, I'm
sure of it.~~
LISL. It only seems that way -- so much has happened.
MOTHER FRANZISKA. Oh, yes, what did I hear --
let me see -- ~~why, certainly,~~ Frau Moeller, the
wife of the newly promoted Captain Moeller.
LISL. Yes, as a matter of fact, that has made a difference in my life -- ~~a great difference -- you
can't imagine.~~

MOTHER FRANZISKA. ~~Perhaps not. But~~ your visit
today?

LISL. It has been a long time, and I thought you would
appreciate, ~~I mean,~~ that you would like to know
what has happened, in the town, ~~I mean.~~

MOTHER FRANZISKA. Oh, we're not isolated here
~~-- a little distance, but not isolation -- The
monastery is old,~~ but we're not living in the
Middle Ages. S→ Cross C(R of desk) K (side)

LISL. I don't mean that. I merely meant ~~that~~ -- your
work here -- the war hasn't changed it that
much. But everything else goes on . . . And
you?

MOTHER FRANZISKA. Me? I go on, and on, ~~and
on.~~

LISL. So you haven't changed either.

MOTHER FRANZISKA. Oh, I have, I suppose -- but
as long as the work goes on, I go on. Smae closer

LISL (uncomfortable). Well, in a way, I expected that.

MOTHER FRANZISKA (direct). Lisl. This conversation is foolish! We're talking to each other like
strangers.

LISL. ~~I don't know what you mean.~~ It's been a long
time . . .

MOTHER FRANZISKA. ~~Come on, now, Lisl,~~ you are S→ L
as uncomfortable as I am with this tedious
conversation. ~~Lisl, we're sisters. Look at me,
remember me?~~

LISL. Oh, Franziska! S→ Chair

MOTHER FRANZISKA. Franziska, not Fritzie? Perhaps you are not my little sister, Lisl, then?

LISL. What I mean, Franziska, ~~I mean,~~ Fritzie, is that

you are making something out of nothing.

MOTHER FRANZISKA. I will speak for myself then. I am uncomfortable with a woman who speaks to me as if she were speaking to a stranger -- passing the time of day. I tell you, I am uncomfortable with that woman -- there, I have spoken for myself. Who are you?

LISL. You are exasperating! You know who I am, and as for your discomfort, I don't know what you mean.

=> S in her face

MOTHER FRANZISKA (taking her hands). Lisl, I'm your big sister Fritzie. We have the same mother and father, remember? We lived in the same house, slept in the same bed, we took baths together, remember? We had a calico cat we called Mouse, remember? And you sit there wringing your hands as if you were on trial.

S close & remain / any gap

L Sit in chair & Sure of self again

LISL. I've changed -- perhaps, that's it. I've grown -- and I'm not your little sister any more.

MOTHER FRANZISKA. Oh, really, you have finally caught up with me, then?

LISL. You know what I mean -- don't be patronizing. You're such a bore when you're patronizing, Fritzie.

MOTHER FRANZISKA. Ah, now I recognize you. My dear Lisl, tell me the truth, before I bore you to death. The truth, please, why are you here?

S => stove

Turn to L

LISL. I came to help -- to help you and the monastery of Maria Morgenstern -- that's all.

Superior attitude

MOTHER FRANZISKA. I'm grateful. But in what

way? We need milk. Can you find us a cow --
or give us the money to buy one? *Gloves off*

LISL. I'm serious, Fritzie, ~~I came to help.~~

MOTHER FRANZISKA. And I'm serious. too. Right
now, what we need most is milk -- ~~the food is
-- not as good as it should be -- if you really
want to help, find us a cow~~ . . .

LISL. ~~Oh, stop it, Fritzie.~~ Now who's playing games,
who's creating distance? You know what I
mean -- I came to help -- with a little good advice.   *S → behind desk   L →* *cross
DSL,* *3|"*

MOTHER FRANZISKA. Advice? (Sits down, attentive to her.) So. I'm listening.

LISL. It is said in town that the sisters here -- I mean,
~~that the monastery, I mean~~ . . .

MOTHER FRANZISKA. You mean me?

LISL. Yes, I mean you. It is said in Baden that you're
not loyal = that you are not completely loyal
to the cause? *Pace DSL*

MOTHER FRANZISKA. Oh?

LISL. I mean that you are not a loyal German . . .

MOTHER FRANZISKA. Who says that? ~~Who says
that?~~ Be specific -- in what way am I not a
loyal German?

LISL. You are not working for the Fatherland . . .
the Third Reich . . .

MOTHER FRANZISKA. That's not the same thing
. . . for me. Be specific, Lisl, in what way am
I not a loyal German?

LISL. You make this very difficult for me. *Turned away*

MOTHER FRANZISKA. I'm sorry for you, ~~then,~~ but
it's not easy for me, either. I've only asked

you to be specific. ~~For God's sake, say what you have to say.~~

LISL. ~~All right,~~ all right, I'll say what I came here to say, and I hope you'll have the good sense to listen.

MOTHER FRANZISKA (returns to her seat, again attentive). Now, as before, I'm listening.

LISL. You are hiding Jews here!

MOTHER FRANZISKA. Is that a question or an accusation?

LISL. It's a statement meant to help, to let you know that . . .

MOTHER FRANZISKA. That's generous of you.

LISL. You do not know. For harboring Jews, the punishment is confiscation -- arrest -- death, and worse than death. For their own good, such people are . . . taken care of . . .

MOTHER FRANZISKA. Disposed of?

LISL. I'll be specific then. Karl Greiner and Maria . .

MOTHER FRANZISKA. Karl and Maria have been gone from Baden for three years -- ~~to Munich.~~

LISL. Yes, and Werner, who travels more than I -- and certainly more than you, tells me that Karl and Maria were arrested in Munich for hiding Jews in their storage room. First they were beaten -- and then, ~~oh, God, it's frighten-ing,~~ they were . . .

MOTHER FRANZISKA. Yes, they were . . .

LISL. Forced to wear badges, the star, the yellow star . . .

MOTHER FRANZISKA. Some of our friends, ~~your friends and mine,~~ Lisl, are wearing that star.

LISL. Forced to wear the star, given Jewish identification papers, Jewish names, identities -- and were sent to the relocation camp at Dachau.

MOTHER FRANZISKA. Karl and Maria, dear good friends! (She is moved.)

LISL. They made them Jews -- and now they will perish . . .

MOTHER FRANZISKA. Karl and Maria -- they made a choice. They'll know how to accept the consequences of that choice.

LISL. But it is not too late for you to make the right choice.

MOTHER FRANZISKA. You are assuming then that the rumors are true?

LISL. I'm not a child -- or a fool, Fritzie, I know your loyalties do not lie with the party . . .

MOTHER FRANZISKA. There's that word again -- loyalty. I don't recognize loyalty to any party that assumes the power to brand and destroy people -- I don't recognize that as any kind of German loyalty I know.

LISL. My God, you are naive. You're living in the Middle Ages if you think this war and the party, and the Third Reich are to be halted by your scruples.

MOTHER FRANZISKA. I'm not responsible for this war -- but I am responsible for myself, my conscience.

LISL. You must stop and think what it will mean to you then -- to this monastery. As the rumors grow, even now, there are orders to search the monastery and to burn it to the ground.

Werner tells me . . .

MOTHER FRANZISKA. Werner is coming here? ~~When?~~

LISL. I'm telling you, warning you. Last night an
order came from Colonel Lauber. The colonel,
himself, he will be coming here to search -- and
to destroy -- Maria Morgenstern.

MOTHER FRANZISKA. How do you know this?

LISL. I think Werner told me, knowing I would come
here to warn you. He doesn't want Colonel
Lauber to find anything when he gets here.

MOTHER FRANZISKA. Tell me, what does he ex-
pect to find?

LISL. Fritzie, surely, if there are sick people, old and
sick, in the hospital, somewhere, someone will
have enough fear to create evidence.

MOTHER FRANZISKA. Who would believe the old
and the sick -- ~~confined to the infirmary?~~
~~Some of them are hardly aware there is a war~~
~~going on -- they are so weak.~~

LISL. That's not the point. They will be believed.
~~It's too bad, but they will be believed. Do you~~
~~understand?~~

MOTHER FRANZISKA. ~~Yes, I understand.~~ (She
turns to the window, pensive, and then turns
back with determination.) No, I do not understand. I do not understand my sister Lisl, who
stands before me to tell me the news of the
town, how life has changed because of the war.
'Too bad,' she says, 'Jews are wearing badges,
our friends are arrested and dragged off to
resettlement camps, ~~our friends and neighbors.~~

~~Too bad~~ things have changed, the war has
changed things. Jews are no longer permitted
to live in Baden -- or anywhere else. Too bad.'

LISL. Please, Fritzie, ~~please~~ . . . *reach across desk*

MOTHER FRANZISKA. I do not understand this --
or you, ~~my dear, ~~ little sister. (She takes *[shake*
her hands.) Do you understand? ~~No~~, no, *off hand*
listen to me. I am not living in the Middle *get up*
Ages, and I know what goes on in the town, *→ DSL*
and I know that the people I trust and care
about do not trust you. ~~They will not, as~~
~~Klaas says, give you the time of day. And I~~
~~know what that means~~ -- that you are no longer *come behind*
part of them -- that you submit . . . *→* *both rows*

LISL. They all submit. You don't hear of any mass *of pa*
uprisings, do you?

MOTHER FRANZISKA. But you believe, cooperate,
and there's the difference. ~~Not much per-~~
~~haps, but a difference. I do not understand~~

LISL. Please, it's important. I can't explain, ~~I can't~~
~~explain . . . I am . . .~~ (She breaks.) Oh, God,
Fritzie, I'm so afraid. *step away*

MOTHER FRANZISKA. So, you're afraid.

LISL. Werner -- so much is expected of him. His *Turn* *back*
position is important -- he's watched . . . We're *to S*
watched and ~~I'm afraid~~ . . .

MOTHER FRANZISKA. Afraid to speak up or do
anything? *cross in front*

LISL. Anything . . . Anything seems disloyal. *of sta*

MOTHER FRANZISKA. ~~So, I see, I'm an embarrass-~~
~~ment to you.~~ My dear Lisl, you are afraid and
I weep for your fears, but I have them too . . .

LISL. What do you know about fear?

MOTHER FRANZISKA. ~~So you think I don't know about fear. You're wrong~~. I'm afraid because every day I take my life into my own hands, into my hands, freely, because, Lisl, I am afraid not to.

LISL. I don't understand.

MOTHER FRANZISKA. It's the only courage I know, the only strength, to do what I do because I'm afraid not to do it. I am afraid of what I would become if I were not to care, not to dare to love enough -- to risk . . .

LISL. Then the rumors are true.

MOTHER FRANZISKA. They are still rumors -- I can't allow myself to fear them.

LISL. Knowing what may happen to you, to Maria Morgenstern? Lisl

MOTHER FRANZISKA. Nothing can happen to me that I do not choose, and as for Maria Morgenstern, it is the House of God -- it's door will not be shut to anyone.

LISL. It's impossible to explain to you.

MOTHER FRANZISKA. No, not at all, you have explained very well. I understand your fears, and I wish I could help. I used to be able to ~~sew buttons on your dresses and help you~~ with your scrawly penmanship and put your hair in curlers. I wish it was that ~~were so~~ easy, ~~to make your fears well, to make you well. I wish I could help.~~

LISL. So do I, ~~oh, so do I.~~

SISTER KLARA (outside the door). Mother Franziska,

Mother, Klaas has returned from the garage . . .
Oh, I'm sorry . . . Frau Moeller, good afternoon.

LISL. Sister Klara, come. I'll be leaving soon.

SISTER KLARA. Mother, I must speak to you . . .

MOTHER FRANZISKA. Yes? ~~You may speak here~~.

SISTER KLARA. Klaas thought you would like to
know that a truck has arrived -- the Gestapo
guards are in the courtyard . . . Colonel Lauber
is here to speak with you.

MOTHER FRANZISKA. Thank you, Sister. He'll
find his way to my office, I'm certain.

SISTER KLARA. Yes, Mother, and about . . .
Vespers?

MOTHER FRANZISKA. Vespers? Yes, the sun
seems to be setting early this evening -- ~~the
fall comes quite quickly after the frost~~. Ring
the bell for Vespers, Sister. It is a special
day, and we must celebrate. ~~Ring the bell,
Sister, and~~ I will be with you before you sing
the *Salve*.

SISTER KLARA. Yes, I'll see that everything is
ready. (She leaves.)

MOTHER FRANZISKA. Now, Lisl, Colonel Lauber
will be here in a moment. He knows we are
sisters. ~~Don't be afraid -- I will not embarrass
you.~~

LISL. Fritzie, it's not that . . . it's just . . .

MOTHER FRANZISKA. Don't be afraid. This is not
the first time Colonel Lauber and I have met
across this desk. Go now, remember not to
fear for me -- I do what I have to do . . .

LISL. And I?

MOTHER FRANZISKA. I cannot answer that for
        you. Goodbye. (LISL prepares to leave as
        COLONEL LAUBER enters.) *Standing*

COLONEL LAUBER. Good day to you, Mother
        Franziska. And, Frau Moeller, my deepest res-
        pect. Am I intruding?

MOTHER FRANZISKA. Not at all, my sister and I
        were finished with our family . . . conference.
        It's good to be together now and then.

COLONEL LAUBER. I'm sure of that -- so, Frau
        Moeller, you will be riding back to Baden?
        You have transportation?

LISL. Yes, of course.

LAUBER. My car is at your service.

LISL. Thank you, but Werner, Captain Moeller gives
        me the car for my visits -- he's so occupied
        these days -- there isn't time for us to come
        together.

LAUBER. A busy man -- and a competent officer.
        My greetings and respect. (He bows as LISL
        leaves.)

MOTHER FRANZISKA (to LISL). Goodbye, it was
        good seeing you, Lisl. *Leave SL*

LAUBER. So, Mother Franziska, I have come to pay
        my respects to you. I must apologize for this
        intrusion. Sergeant Heimlich, such a bungler,
        all zeal and no tact, reported to me what
        happened this morning. My apologies for his
        clumsiness in handling a really very routine
        situation.

MOTHER FRANZISKA. Will you be seated, Colonel
        Lauber?

LAUBER. No, thank you. This is an official visit.

(The bell rings for Vespers. Slowly from the corners of
	the stage, SISTERS gather in the chapel area
	US. They are seen only in silhouette. Through
	the following scene, the evening service con-
	tinues mimed in quiet movements with chanting
	just audible in the background. MOTHER
	FRANZISKA and COLONEL LAUBER are
	lighted DS in front of this scene.)

MOTHER FRANZISKA. I, myself, have something of
	official business to attend to. I hope it will
	not take too long. The Vesper bell has rung --
	today is a special feast, and I must be there to
	celebrate.
LAUBER. Mother Franziska, outside in the courtyard
	my men are waiting for a signal from me. At
	that signal, they will enter this convent, search,
	and if necessary, destroy, to find the Jews you
	have hidden here. You can avert that scene if
	you give them up.
MOTHER FRANZISKA. Colonel, your threats do not
	frighten me. If Maria Morgenstern can survive
	barbarian invasions, it can survive the Gestapo
	guards.
LAUBER. I ask you to be more cautious, with due
	respect. I ask you to be more cautious. But
	if you choose to be foolish, you will regret it.
MOTHER FRANZISKA. Another threat?
LAUBER. I am prepared to destroy whatever needs
	to be destroyed to prove my point -- my

threat, if you will

MOTHER FRANZISKA. On what grounds?

LAUBER. Jews! There are Jews here! And I have
been charged with ridding the town -- and the
countryside of the Jews! It is an order for
me -- and as for you, you have no choice.

MOTHER FRANZISKA. I cannot take orders from
the Gestapo. The prioress of the monastery of
Maria Morgenstern has been -- and still is, the
only authority within these walls. Check the
town charter -- 1294 A.D. -- Mother Wilhelmina
and Frederic I.

LAUBER. The Third Reich does not recognize such
a charter.

MOTHER FRANZISKA. That's your problem. I am
the authority in this place. Surely, you, of
all people, can understand authority.

LAUBER. I understand the authority by which these
orders operate.

MOTHER FRANZISKA. And I do not. You are on
holy ground -- tread with care.

LAUBER. With all due respect, Mother Franziska, I
warn you, cooperate. It will be for your own
good.

MOTHER FRANZISKA. I'll be the judge of that. You
will not desecrate these halls and corridors.
You will remember where you are.

LAUBER. And you will remember who you are. Do
not think you can intimidate me.

MOTHER FRANZISKA. I am not playing games. I
am stating a position, stating a right. The
monastery of Maria Morgenstern is not under

the jurisdiction of the town, the state -- it
never has been. It is certainly outside the authority of the Gestapo.

LAUBER. You have no rights -- that the Gestapo
recognizes, remember that. ~~No, you will not
win here.~~ You sent Sergeant Heimlich back to
headquarters with his tail between his legs.
You will not do that to me.

MOTHER FRANZISKA. Leave anyway you wish,
but please leave.

LAUBER. I will not leave without the search, with or
without your permission. There will be a
search . . . and . . . the consequences . . . unless,
of course, you produce the Jews you are hiding.

MOTHER FRANZISKA. You are assuming there are
Jews here.

LAUBER. ~~We know there are Jews here.~~ Klaas
Hoeffler has been watched. Not all people in
Baden are so loyal to you here. ~~He has been
watched and has been reported and everything
leads to you, to this place.~~ We know that you
have been hiding Jews -- children -- through the
underground to the border. It has only been a
matter of time -- as the last Jews were arrested,
as the ghetto was cleared, that the path would
lead to you . . . ~~We know.~~

MOTHER FRANZISKA. You are mistaken. You
will find only the sick here . . . a few still left
in the infirmary.

LAUBER. Do you wish to turn over the Jews now,
or will you force me to search this place?
Will you take responsibility for what happens

in that search?
MOTHER FRANZISKA. The sisters are in the chapel
          now, the search would be useless.
LAUBER. On the contrary, that will insure that they
          will be occupied with their prayers and out of
          our way. When we have finished with our
          search, we will find the Jews. I will not return
          to my commandant without them. And you,
          Mother Franziska, will not stand in my way.
          (He goes to the window and signals to the
          guards in the courtyard below.)

(There is a shuffle of feet, orders heard in the distance.
          In the darkness US, the guards enter searching,
          circling the chapel area, but never entering.
          The scene is played very slowly in dim light.)

LAUBER. Now, I have time to wait.
MOTHER FRANZISKA. I must leave you then --
          for Vespers.
LAUBER. I think not. Tonight you will have to ex-
          cuse yourself.
MOTHER FRANZISKA. Not tonight, of all nights.
          It's a special feast, a celebration.
LAUBER. They will have to celebrate without you,
          Mother Franziska. You will remain here with
          me.   Until we are interrupted . . . when my
          men have found what we came to find.
MOTHER FRANZISKA. You are so certain then?
LAUBER. So certain.
MOTHER FRANZISKA (at her desk, attempts to
          continue her work, alert to the sounds of the

search and the soft chanting in the background.
Abruptly the chanting stops. She rises startled.)
Excuse me, I must make sure Sister Klara has
what she needs for . . .

LAUBER (stops her). You will, please, remain here.

(In the background the chapel scene is changing. The
sisters have stopped chanting. With solemn
steps, DAVID walks to the center of the
chapel, opens the large scriptures and reads
slowly, pointing to each word as he reads.
He closes the book solemnly and speaks to
the group, gesturing. His final gesture is to
speak the blessing with open arms. As this
scene is taking place inside the chapel, the
GESTAPO GUARDS come nearer and nearer,
circling the chapel, approaching, but never
entering. At the end, DAVID embraces
MIRIAM and the SISTERS warmly. KLAAS
approaches and they are seen to be making
preparations to leave, visibly aware that the
searching GUARDS are just outside the chapel.)

MOTHER FRANZISKA (aware only of the long
silence and visibly relieved when she hears the
Salve). Vespers has ended . . . the sisters will
be returning to their work . . . the sick in the
infirmary . . . the sister have work to do.

LAUBER. We will not disturb the sick. My guess is
that we will have evidence before we need to
do that.

MOTHER FRANZISKA. You have already disturbed

all of us.

LAUBER. It was your choice. You chose to be --
shall we say, uncooperative?

MOTHER FRANZISKA. I chose to be firm. You are
an intruder.

LAUBER. Nevertheless, your lack of cooperation will
be noted, and reported . . .

MOTHER FRANZISKA. And then?

LAUBER. Surely you do not think you can claim
immunity -- this is the Twentieth Century.

MOTHER FRANZISKA. You know as well as I what
this monastery means to this town . . .

LAUBER. The people, your friends, will not lift a
finger to help you, unless they too wish to be
-- arrested.

MOTHER FRANZISKA. I am not so sure of that.

LAUBER. Don't count on these walls to protect you.
There is a new order here, loyalty to the
Third Reich. The people are loyal to us . . .
and if not loyal . . . there is always fear.

MOTHER FRANZISKA. You wield that weapon well.

LAUBER. It is persuasive. I would advise you to
consider it, as a possible solution to the inevit-
able confrontations between us.

SEARGEANT HEIMLICH (entering). Sir, we have
searched -- throughout the premises. There
does not seem to be any evidence.

LAUBER. Are you sure, Sergeant?

HEIMLICH. Yes, Sir. We have searched everywhere.
And now, finally, the chapel.

LAUBER. And you report?

HEIMLICH. Nothing, Sir, there is nothing to report.

LAUBER. Nothing? Impossible! I will see for myself.
Dismissed!

HEIMLICH. Yes, Sir. (He leaves.)

LAUBER (to MOTHER FRANZISKA). I will leave,
for now, but we will find what we came to
find. Remember that. It may help you to
develop a little fear. ~~Yes, a little salutary fear
will be helpful to you — and to Maria Morgenstern.~~

MOTHER FRANZISKA. Tell me, Colonel Lauber,
what should I fear?

LAUBER. You should fear for your very lives. I say
it again, you are not immune. The orders are
clear, the Jewish pestilence must be swept
away, the Fatherland cleansed, scorched, if
necessary, but they will be destroyed.

MOTHER FRANZISKA. So history repeats itself,
destruction by fire, conquest by holocaust.

LAUBER. It has been efficient in the past; it will
serve us now.

MOTHER FRANZISKA. And Maria Morgenstern?

LAUBER. I do not hesitate to set fire to the walls myself. My orders are just that – set fire, destroy
That which what cannot be subjugated.

MOTHER FRANZISKA (the *Salve* is just ending).
Subjugated? Listen, ~~listen~~, quiet Vesper song
in the dusky evening air -- it's been going on
for centuries here -- ~~it can't mean much to
destroy so simple a beauty.~~

LAUBER. I'm not so sure it is that simple. That is
what I am here to find out. It may be that it
is quite deceptive -- for its own purposes.

MOTHER FRANZISKA. No, I think not. The truth
        is very simple -- we are what we are . . .
LAUBER. That remains to be seen . . .
MOTHER FRANZISKA. And more important, we do
        what we must do.
LAUBER. I will remember that.

(The Vesper bell starts to ring slowly, solemnly. She
        goes to the window and looks out towards
        the border, returning to end the meeting.)

MOTHER FRANZISKA. The evening star seems es-
        pecially bright tonight. (Sighs and returns to
        her work.) Well, Colonel . . .?
LAUBER. I will be leaving . . . for now. (He salutes.)
MOTHER FRANZISKA. That bells tells me the sisters
        have left the chapel. You may wish to stop
        there, Colonel. It may give you peace.
LAUBER. Good evening, then. (Bows, salutes and
        turns.)

(MOTHER FRANZISKA waits until he leaves and runs
        to the window. The Vesper bells are chiming
        loudly. KLAAS, DAVID and MIRIAM are seen
        US making their escape to the border. With a
        quickening pace, the bells gradually fill the
        stage with sound. MOTHER FRANZISKA
        takes the old school bell from her desk and
        starts to ring it boldly, cheerfully. As the sound
        is heard, the chapel bells pick up the rhythm and
        movement of her joyous ringing. She stands C
        ringing the bell with both hands, her head thrown

back joyfully, as the chapel chimes join her
jubilantly, and the LIGHTS fade to BLACK.)

END OF PLAY